twist

BRUCE PARKINSON SPANG

Art Copyright © 2025 by Liz Kalloch
Cover image: detail of What the Body Remembers
Title page: detail of Winged
© + dedication pages: detail of Before the Frost
Section One: detail of Hypatia
Section Two: detail of Edge
Section Three: detail of Aurora
Section Four: detail of Unfurl

ISBN: 978-1-966343-36-3 (Hard Cover)
          978-1-966343-37-0 (Soft Cover)

Spang. bruce
Twist

Edited by: Amy Klein

Warren publishing

Published by WARREN Publishing
Charlotte, NC
www.warrenpublishing.net
Printed in the United States

To my loving husband and lifemate, Myles Rightmire,
for his support, insight, and understanding, and to Alice Person,
my dear friend, confidant, and publisher for many years

PRAISE FOR TWIST

"... each poem is an evocation full of the texture of life, yet seen through the honest lens of time ... All this makes for an exceptionally moving and wise book, one that, in wearing its humility lightly, winds up at poetry's basic location–a feeling of pity for our misconceptions and awe for the physical world in which we find ourselves and the love we can manifest within that world."

–Baron Wormser, *The History Hotel*

"*Twist* is Bruce Spang's love song to time. ... Spang explores with great sensitivity the perplexity and wonder of coming out in midlife ... This book is rich in compassion and insight, as well as those lovely evocative moments when Spang hints at a future loss of time–but not yet, not here in 'this living, this late lingering light.'"

–Betsy Sholl, *As If a Song Could Save You*

"These tender poems animate love and regret, sorrow and shame, gilding them with hard-won, patient generosity."

–Dawn Potter, *Accidental Hymn*

"There is a mindfulness common to all the emotionally moving and lyrically precise poems in this collection as they reflect upon past memories of longing and spiritual homecoming. ... The cosmopolitan, mature voice of Bruce Spang is both an authentic and original one, and Twist deserves shelf space next to Ted Kooser's best."

–Dan Guenther, *The Crooked Truth*

"'… a brave collection that speaks to surviving conformist expectations of childhood, career, and marriage, while knowing all along there was 'a question I could / not outrace no matter how far / I ran from myself …' In poems that ache with restraint and yearning, Spang reveals the confusion of growing up gay in an inadmissible era …."

–Kenneth Chamlee, *The Best Material for the Artist in the World*

"The current coursing through Bruce Spang's poems–*Twist*–flows with extraordinary compassion. … what makes this collection especially moving is the sensitivity with which Spang treats all his men. Because this is, ultimately, a book about men. And aspects of love."

– Marie Harris, *Desire Lines*

"In Bruce Spang's new collection, Twist, the title becomes a definitive turn to a celebration of identity after a childhood constrained by the expectations of a boy growing up in the 1950s. … But the collection is also full of a longing to be loved and to live authentically.'"

– Ellen Bass, *Indigo*

OTHER BOOKS BY BRUCE PARKINSON SPANG

Poetry

All You'll Derive: A Caregivers Journey, 2020
Not Just Anybody, BPS Books, 2015
Boy at the Screen Door, Moon Pie Press, 2014
To the Promised Land Grocery, Moon Pie Press, 2008
The Knot, Snow Drift Press, 2006

Poetry Chapbooks

Tip End of Time, Smyle Publications, 2005
Once the First Berries Dissolve, 2003

Poetry Anthologies

Passion and Pride: Poets in Support of Equality, Moon Pie Press, 2012
I Have Walked Through Many Lives, Young Voices–Scarborough,
  Moon Pie Press, 2009

Libretto

Reckoning, the Musical, 2010

Novels

The River Crossed, Wisdom House Press, 2024
Those Close Beside Me, Piscataqua Press, 2018
The Deception of the Thrush, Piscataqua Press, 2014

Memoir

Those Close Beside Me; A Young Man's Search for Home, 2025
No Way Back: A Young Man's Search for Home. Piscataqua Press, 2025

CONTENTS

II

Regard the freedom of seventy years ago.
It is no longer air. The houses still stand
though they are rigid in rigid emptiness.

III

Even our shadows, their shadows, no longer remain.

IV

It is an illusion that we were ever alive,
lived in the house of mothers, arranged ourselves
by our own motions in the freedom of air.

It is an illusion that we were ever alive,
Lived in the house of mothers, arranged ourselves
By our own motions in the freedom of air.

Regard the freedom of seventy years ago.
It is no longer air. The houses still stand,
Though they are rigid in rigid emptiness.

Even our shadows, their shadows, no longer remain.
The lives these lived in the mind are at an end.

– From "The Rock," by Wallace Stevens

Poem with a Line from Lorca

Out in the sky no one sleeps. No one. No one.
No one sleeps. *

Yet here I am, old friend, still here.
The wind leans against the window.
The mottled-faced Chihuahua nestles
under my arm, snoozing. At my feet
my lover deep in a dream slumbers.
The air from the furnace hums
in the grate a soft warm tune.

If there are stars, they are waking now.
A fox crouches by the shrub on the hillside,
his ears alert to the vole scurried out of its burrow.
There is a shriek. A silence. A satiety.

If tomorrow will come back unhurried
and reside in the doorway of yesterday,
we can rest inside an hour's arm,
curled like a leaf on the stem of night.
No one. No one is listening. Not one.

The night will find us. Ready yet wary.
Our arms, full of yearning, reach out.
The sky whispers, "I'm here. Wait
for me" as if it, too, wanted to be held.

The wind has nothing more to say.
Oh, Lorca, who has taken you
to the field, barren and dry, and told
you to kneel and cry out in a voice
distinct and clear, we can still hear,
"No one. No one. No one sleeps."

*From "Sleepless City" (Brooklyn Bridge Nocturne) by Federico García Lorca

One

THE LIVES THESE LIVED
IN THE MIND ARE AT AN END.

Tutorial

When Michael asked if I'd ever French-kissed a girl,
I pondered him, parked across from me
on a picnic table, his legs straddling
the seat, the late afternoon sun
soft on his face, his eyes gazing intently
at me, and replied, "No," almost ashamed
at how little I'd done.

"Have you?" I asked.
"Yeah, it feels great," he said.

I didn't want to be a bother,
yet asked, "How do you do it?"
"Let me show you," he said,
scooting closer to me.

Our knees touched. He leaned forward,
pressing his lips to mine,
sticking his tongue in my mouth.

I recoiled. "Don't be such a girl," he said.

His hands on my hips; mine on his.
He slid his tongue in and out,
up and down, as if he knew exactly
what to do, as if spelunking for something
in me that would take forty years to emerge,
delving into me, until, in response to his
tongue's longing, my tongue joined in,
that slow waltz. Mine nuzzled next
to his, as if we were translating another
language, like French, its soft vowels swelling
up in my mouth as if I understood every word.

The Door When It Opens

Why do I always go back to sex?
I return to it as though to a door
through which I can find myself.

I place my hand on the doorknob,
yet it's locked. I knock. No one
is there. Yet here I am waiting.

The clock in the hallway chimes.
If I stay put, stand here, I will
find someone else is there

waiting with me, the two of us
inches apart, his breath warm,
titillating the hairs on my neck.

He has been here long before
time was invented, before the sky
was blue, before I sensed

tomorrow is a gift given today.
Maybe it wasn't sex after all.
Such a funny word with its 's'

and 'x' as if, by itself, sex could
erase itself. Only the 'e' is there,
holding them together, wanting

them to be tender, to be loved
as I do, as I have always wanted
the door to creak open

to find that home.

The Child of Frankenstein

I was supposed to be the monster.
Father stuffed the *Chicago Tribune*
inside my jacket and slipped the khaki-
colored mask with its oozing wound
over my head.

With each inhalation,
rubber stuck to my nose. The slits
for eyeholes compacted the view
as if I were gazing out a camera's lens
at Mom grimacing and Father
laughing, "That's my boy!" He showed
me how to walk stiff-legged with arms
like pistons back and forth and to go
"Grrr. Grrr" if anyone asked who I was.

Following the big boys, door-to-door,
I went, "Grrr. Grrr." Our neighbors
weren't fooled. "Oh, Brucie, how cute,"
they said. "What a big head you have."
Tootsie Rolls plopped in my bag,
calories accumulating, my sweets,
my sweets, my sweet rewards.

The mask, clamped to my neck
like the helmet of a diving suit,
with a peephole for air, kept
my breath inside, scorching
my sweaty face, until my eyes stung.

I wanted to be me, a third grader
who lived at 10 Arlington Avenue,
sang in a choir, wore a white
robe; a boy with buckteeth,
a crewcut, and a body mom
called "husky," who couldn't
scare a fly off his nose, couldn't
wait to yank off his mask,
spread candy on his bed.

That night Father set the mask
on my dresser. Its empty slots
for eyes stared at me as if that face
wanted to be stitched to my face.
For decades, I was still that child,
even with my own room, my own
bed, so afraid that mask became him.

What We Remembered When Father Lay Dying

Between my parents' bedroom and ours,
there was a long, knee-high cubby hole
tall enough for suitcases

my brother and I could crawl into to peer
out at our father's pale body in boxer shorts
strewn on the bed, his mouth agape

snoring big looping guttural snorts that startled
flies hovering above his head. His bean-pole
legs and string-bean arms lay spread out

as if he'd fallen from
an enormous height. If he knew
we were watching him, he'd tan

our hides like he did if we refused
to eat our beans. At our naptime,
he snatched and lugged us

under his arms like sacks
of dirt. Up flipped down,
near ripped far. Three steps

at a time, he ascended, then
flung us on our beds. Quiet time–
that's when the giant napped.

So we crept close to him.
The floor creaked. His eyelids
fluttered. We dared not touch.

Mother had warned us, "Don't disturb
your father, or else it will be hell
to pay." Yet there we were,

not after bags of gold,
not even a golden harp
that could lull him to sleep forever.

We craved to be close
to his quivering lips,
to peek inside his dreams–

Did he dream of his three-piece suits,
or dressing us for success in
Brooks Brothers navy blazers?

Did he dream of climbing the corporate ladder
to grab the keys to the kingdom
instead of getting stuck as vice president?

Or did he dream of us, parts of
his ambition machine out of reach,
outdoing him? In his dreams, did

we endure the snarl of his rage
when we didn't do as he said,
"Dinner time, bedtime,"

like the clock was a command?
We liked him being quiet, still.
Half a lifetime later, with tubes stuffed

in his nose, monitors at his
bedside, mouth drooped,
breath uneven, no longer a man

to spit commands, but frail
at the end of life's stalk,
he gazed at us and wondered who

had axed his heart
that would last two
days. No fairy-tale giant,

but a shrunken has-been
in his hospital bed, his skin
a yellowish gold in the after light

of an afternoon in March, he asked,
"Have I lived a good life?"
as if we were the final arbiters

of this body we could have lifted into the air
and, if we had let go, would have floated
out the window into clouds.

A good life? we thought. *What's that?*
A man who had a Lincoln Continental
under a palm tree? That he had.

Who had a martini at boom-boom hour
every day? By all means. Yes.
A man who was a seeker of truth?

He had to be kidding.
But he asked again as if we could
forget his swats, slaps, and insults.

What dared we say–
there beside the body
as its heart gave out?

Bill of Rights

"OK, Mr. Spang, your turn."
Words stick together, nouns bump into verbs,
multisyllables like Do Not Enter signs entangle
my tongue. He gives me the next word. I repeat
it and read on and stutter again. He gives me
es-tab-lish-ment. I pronounce it. I carry on—
"of religion, or prohibiting the free exercise
thereof; or abridging the freedom of speech,"
as if this amendment were meant for me
in the furthest seat in the back row of the class.
                    "There you go," says
broad-shouldered Mr. Armstrong with his fat,
phantasmagoric tie, and his stout finger
pointing at me, nodding at every word while
he glares at guffaws, desk by desk,
shaking his head almost as if he must have
known, once I eased into words, no law,
no one could silence me. They'd become
mine, like the candies in the glass jar
on the desk, the ones I could gather
anytime, unwrap their cellophane,
feel their hard sweetness on my tongue.

Spanking

I wait in the closet,
stiff, standing beneath
the shirts on hangers,
lifeless, sleeves slung

down as if in sympathy
before the thud of shoes,
the pressed slacks there,
upright, before me—his finger

points "Bend over"—
his belt unloosened
like a slick tongue,
folded, lifted.

Gravity does the rest:
how any object flung
into space comes back
with a ferocity—simple

physics, of branding wrong
on wrong until parting. He pats
my head "That's it," leaves
me to wince, pull up my pants,

and waddle into the room
where at night I wake and see,
deep in the closet, a boy, pants
down, who will not come out.

Unbecoming a Man

We were teens. "The boys," our parents called us.
We sat at the Formica table in the kitchen.
Steve's mother, cutting the BLTs in half, stood
at a counter a few feet from us.

Steve opened the *Playboy* centerfold, spreading it
out like a map with directions to the promise of manhood,
and pointed at Miss December in a Santa Claus hat
and nothing else, sitting on a sleigh as if she wanted us
to give her a push. Steve giggled and did as men do—
pointed at her breasts and whispered, "Look at THOSE!"

They looked like overinflated
balloons that, if she wasn't careful, might lift her off
the sled and carry her off to the swanky boudoir of Mr. Hefner
who'd do what men do.

I studied them and glanced at his mother
who was also inspecting them and
cutting the BLTs into fourths and, I suspected,
had Steve pointed to the woman's faint crop of pubic hair,
would have sliced the BLTs into eighths and sixteenths
until they were only crumbs, bits of bacon,
scraps of lettuce with drops of mayonnaise,
and the bloody stump of a tomato.

Steve caught her glare, winked at me
as if we shared some secret, folded Miss
December undercover, and placed the magazine
on the table between us like a passport to a fantasy island
where in five, in ten years we'd wash up, randy
and ready to play with Miss June who, debarking
Hefner's yacht, The Southern Cross, in her tennis shoes,
would be even more eager to play with us.

But a riptide had already dragged
me far out to sea, in a rudderless
skiff, in another direction.

Fever Unbroken

Sweat drenched my body. There was
no shade. Mother, right by my side,

propped the pillows behind me,
patted my head with a cool cloth.

"There, there, you'll be all right."
Her voice pleading as if in

a prayer. Leaning next to me,
she read *Robinson Crusoe*,

his being on the beach, the relentless
sun, wave on wave of emptiness.

Cold compresses pressed on my head.
I flipped and turned, not on sand

but in a street where bricks, slabs,
windows crashed, buildings like dominoes

smashed over me. *Get off. Get off*.
Vicks VapoRub slathered on my chest,

a thick comforter tucked to my chin,
trapped inside pajamas buttoned to the neck,

debris all around me. Mother bawled my name.
Even father sat beside my bed, squinted into my eyes

as if searching for the two dead brothers
before me–the one mother found in a crib,

no breath; the other, unnamed, no pulse.
Father stayed for hours, days. My hand in his,

he said, "Get better, Son. Your mom worries."
It was days, but I did as he asked as I

always did, returned like newly made,
spry, busy about the house by day,

and by night to my bed beside my living
brother. We kept breathing as if

to apologize for our dead brothers whose
claim on us was the door to our room

that every night had always been open
so our parents could hear our breathing.

The Tiny Boy Speaks

You needn't be afraid of me,
my tiny body
that big people pick up
and toss in the air

where I can spread my arms
into a word I've begun to know–
transcendence–
while you're stuck here on Earth.

I'm standing on a dock.
Water hushes the pilings below me.
My eyes squint in the bright noonday blare.

Do you remember me?

I'm looking far off to the left,
my lips set tight, hands folded in front of me
as in prayer, listening to something–is it
my brother or mother–or is it
the screen door slamming in the wind?

You want to know if there is
any way to get back inside me,
to be on this dock in my body.

You want to have only Classic Comics
to read–*The Swiss Family Robinson*–
in your tree house with a python clutching your leg.
You want to clear shelves of books you should've read.
You want to be comforted and look out the bedroom's
open window at our parents who sit in wicker chairs,
facing the lake with its mouth around the moon.

Insistent, you ask if you can be me again.
I wish I could help. The trick might be
to let me turn around, walk to the end
of the dock (I'm not afraid of water),
and let me leap into the lake,
for–remember?–I can swim.

You can follow me, just the two of us,
pushing out past the boat
with one oar left in the water,
past the raft where mother rests,
to a place where memory ceases to matter,
where you, the man; and I, the child,
swim into oneness.

A Summer Without Mosquitoes

At the camp cottage on Lake Wawasee
where the night leaned over the water and
oil lamps on porches flickered,
the DDT truck would rumble by and
spray bellows of smoke that rose and spread
over lawns, bushes, cottages, and Lake.

We would race behind those bellows,
let the sour-sweet odor cast over us,
assured mosquitoes (if any were left)
would never touch us. For
hundreds of yards, not a bee,
a fly, a moth, a spider stirred.

There must have been carcasses for miles.
Rachel Carson with the tumor buried
in her breast would later write about the silence
of chickadees, cardinals, robins, blue jays,
and wrens. But in 1954, all was just fine.

We could sit on an unscreened porch,
never swat the summer long, never once
inquire what we had inhaled. We were happy.
My brother, quick of foot, outraced me.
"Hurry, slow poke." We plowed into clouds
of smoke, bare-chested, unbitten,
then jogged back to our cabin to pray,
"Our father," and sleep deep into

the unscreened night, secure we lived
in a nation of people like us, we two
white boys chasing our sweet poison
as if nothing could ever, would ever,
be so much fun as racing
after what was killing us.

My Father, There Was a Time

When the lamps dimmed and voices,
after a flurry of words, diminished;
when my father said, "We should be headed
back;" when father came to wake my brother,
who rose and staggered to the door, and me.

I curled deep into myself. My father nudged me.
"Come on, time to go," but I didn't stir.
He picked me up. I nestled into his shoulder,
my head nudged on his neck into the day-long
stubble and scent of Old Spice and whiskey.

Down the stairs to the car, mother driving,
the lurch of rut, the turn and counterturn,
and long curve to the other side of the lake
as, jarred awake, I caught sight of the swollen
moon, spread out, at the water's edge.

Then the ignition key clicked. Father
rose and, step by step, climbed to
the screen door, and the eight stairs
to our room where, one hand under my arm,
the other on my rump, he laid me down.

My clothes peeled off, one arm up, next
the other, one leg up, then another,
my skin electric under the warmth
of his hand. My PJs pulled over and up
and on, I nestled under covers.

He kissed my lips, patted my chest,
"Sweet dreams, my son." There,
then my dreams were sweet
because all I ever wanted
was to be a son in his arms.

The Comfort of Elms

A hundred feet tall, sixty feet wide,
row on row clear down the street,
six blocks from our front door
on Arlington Avenue to the First

Congregation Church, elms,
their arching canopy a cathedral.
Slivers of light cast on shoulders,
shade stretched curb to curb

as my brother and I strode to keep
up with father, long-legged, ahead of us.
Mom clasped my hand. "Be quicker."
I wanted to be still like understory

beneath vast green vaults and buttresses,
not confined inside of stained-glass
shimmerings. I wanted light to extend
upward as if the whole august world

reached up, grasped at the apex
that rose to bless everything—
yet one summer as if someone
could unwind creation, one upper

branch, then two, seemed scorched
by red-hot irons. Leaves burned up,
clumps withered. This disease
held the hisses of venomous snakes.

Soon street by street, our elms,
their guts eaten by beetles, thirsted
without water, starved without food,
fell dead. I saw men with chainsaws

delimb them, sever them branch
by branch, cut them down, section by
section, heap them by roadsides
like war-torn sanctuaries. Even the

hapless sky abandoned as if faith,
deracinated, was carting away
my childhood–nothing left
but that blue scar to comfort me.

Two

REGARD THE FREEDOM OF
SEVENTY YEARS AGO.

IT IS NO LONGER AIR. THE
HOUSES STILL STAND

THOUGH THEY ARE RIGID IN
RIGID EMPTINESS.

Open Window in a Vacant Room

The past has never happened—
who I was and what I felt, even
this carpet with its smudge of sun,
this cat curled on the couch,
these words that trail across my mind
like memory's allure, gone.

I am a certain erasure, ephemeral,
a fiction whom even I have forgotten,
the way, for only one week, the brilliant tangerine
of sugar maple foliage blazes the hillside.
Yet photographers still stand under them,
their cameras' mouths snapping
to swallow what was already gone.

Are the box of love letters we cast in the fire,
our home at the corner of River Road
and Longley Lane where a dog
yelped at anyone who walked by,
like these leaves heaved on pavement
and crushed by traffic?

Let go. Let go, they whisper.
I kick them. They topple, unlike
themselves, nothing
anyone would photograph,
yet there they are under my feet.
Still here, they say, *still here*.

The Day Marilyn Died

In the basement, I was singing along with Pat Boone's "Love Letters in the Sand." I had loose slacks on because, if I wore jeans, I felt that my big thighs would rip the seams. My body, what little I knew of it, was ugly. But I could sing. I belted the lines, "On a day like today we passed the time away," and felt strangely sad. I had dated a girl once, but it was a disaster. Nothing happened. I had no idea what to do or what to say to her. She asked me, "What's wrong with you?" and I wished I could have answered. I knew so little then. No one was home. Mother, off to bridge club, had left a note: *Be home later. Dinner in fridge*. Then the radio announced that Marilyn Monroe was dead. I cried. My head bowed, my hands on the sink, gripping it as if the drain were sucking me down. The dirty dishes piled there. I bawled. It felt as if someone had ripped out my chest. I had seen her white halter dress like angels' wings blown high by a subway train passing under a grate. I had heard her sing "Happy Birthday" to the president in a white-sequined gown that looked as if it had been shrink-wrapped onto her. Her soft, breathy voice with its little giggle seemed so genuine. I wished she had sung it for me, for a sixteen-year-old boy who loved her as much as he had loved anyone. I could see her sashay over to me and cradle my head in her hand and say, "You're lovely really." She would press her lips to mine. "Don't worry," she would say. "Your thighs are perfect. Look how strong you are!" She would put her hands on them. I would lean over, pull her down next to me, both of us kneeling like two people praying. I would point to the sand where I had written, *I LOVE YOU*. "Oh, my!" she would say. "I love you too." For that moment, the pills on her dresser, her corpse on the bed, the torn fabric of her life, ceased to matter. The acne cream in my pocket, the unmade bed of my life, and the Pat Boone song I was singing—"How you laughed when I cried each time I saw the tide …"—all became slits of light streaming through the basement windows, drenching us like a blessing. We were as happy as two lonely people could be.

– Song quotes from "Love Letters in the Sand" by Pat Boone

The Wilderness

My brother, a traveling salesman, after
years of endless drives from Denver
to South Bend, Bangor to St. Pete,
bought a noise machine to help him sleep.

It played waves of an ocean coming in,
crashing, and pulling back. There was
the rain splattering on the pavement;
the roof; the car, its exertion, its restlessness
undiminished for hours.
                              But it was the sound of
a train clicking on the tracks that worked
for him, the train—always on the move—
passing houses in the dark, with one dim lamp
in the window, then passing only the rare
lights in car windows, the clicky-click
all night long by malls, by hillsides,
into forests, around lakes, and over
rivers where he used to ride as a kid
with his trunk packed by our mother
with swimsuit, undies, T-shirts,
jacket—nametag on each

          to Rodney Kroeler YMCA camp
on the crest of a ridge overlooking a languid lake.
He'd be, back then, king of the tether ball
court and ski, slalom, bending his knees
to leap the wakes, and sleep alone by
the screen windows, and hear the lapping
of the lake and loons, crickets and frogs,
the soft air of moonlight on his forehead,
               back before adulthood's
raw and endless nights with the traffic
of the every day too near him—I saw
his sour marriage, his dead-end career,
his two bankruptcies—and felt the fear
that kept him restless, awake,
               wanting to latch onto
success with his fists, to keep
running, to carry himself far away
with a clickety-clack of night,
where he never arrives, only passes
one station after another, deep
into the wilderness of night.

Remember, Michael

in that swimming pool dressing room
when three older boys stripped?

Each had pubic hair and pencil-lined fuzz up
to their navels. We had few hairs–

wiry question marks. The guys laughed
as one grabbed the other guy's cock

as if he owned it. They told how
they got caught jacking off.

We never got caught, but knew
what we did was no laughing

matter because, although our lives
went on–both married with kids–

we sensed something drew us together
that wasn't just playing around.

I heard you went to our 30th high school
reunion, flamboyant as always,

letting yourself be. Ten years later
at our 40th, Craig, a used car salesman,

told me, "Michael weirded me out,
acted like a fairy–you know, limp wrists,

the whole fag thing. Everyone laughed.
What was wrong with him?

A month later, big news. Sad really.
He blew his brains out. A waste."

Wrong. A simple word like bullet.
It doesn't mean to harm.

I'm talking to you, Michael, before
you go to the basement,

before you check the chambers
of the revolver, before the cool metal

touches your temple, before you grasp
the trigger in your soft, gentle hand.

I'm speaking to you because I remember
your hand, the bed we sat on,

and the way you caressed my body
as if to bless it. If only I'd been there

beside Craig at our 30th, I wouldn't
laugh nor try to fit in anymore.

I would take you aside, look you
in the eye, and know our lives

depend on what we dared not
say, the love we never spoke.

Spitting the Seeds

Teenagers, the first chance we get,
my brother and I take our red chunks
of watermelon with hundreds of seeds,
outside, and draw a line on the deck.

What is freedom if not being able to spit
as far as you want? The trick is to place
a black seed on your tongue flat,
purse your lips, take a long inhalation

curl your tongue's tip, angle the seed
up, but not too high, until it's lodged behind
your teeth, then let it fly. Some flop
like a failed launch. Some veer sideways.

Some fling like righteousness across the deck.
My brother bolts after a good one, scores
with chalk the place it splattered. "There it is!
That's the bestest yet," he says. "Beat that."

I huff and puff one seed after another.
Tilting my head back, I imagine
I'm at the launch pad at Cape Canaveral
and President Kennedy, in his sunglasses,

sees I am his kind of guy—full of vigor—
as my missile splits the air toward
the farthest edge of the deck. It's a perfect
trajectory on that hot afternoon, not unlike

that day in Birmingham, not a month before,
right there on the nightly news, when fire
hoses swatted Black kids with the force
of cannons. Those Black teens have crossed
a line between the now and yet to be.

Meanwhile, my slick little seed is
is rising with nothing in its way,
not a tank, no Bull Connor barking
"Take 'em down," just the pure suburban sky

and my brother on his feet saying, "No way.
No way." The seed, still rising, clears
the deck and is still, as far as I know, rising.
There are moments when all I have lost,

all I could have silenced, returns
as the portent of seeds in my mouth,
seeds that, loaded just right, could make anyone
feel as if nothing was, and nobody could stop them.

I am still watching those kids, hundreds of them,
row after row, the leaders of change, stepping
out of the 16th Street Baptist Church,
and marching onto Kelly Ingram Park

to face the batons, rifles, and hate as if nothing,
nothing can keep them from moving on. I can
still hear their voices rising, singing,
"Freedom, freedom" as they go.

Man on the Walkway at Evening

The men who pass by our lodge
walking–how strange–
alone or side by side

on a road singularly
untrafficked
this time of day

and others
some of whom I've loved
who are miles

even years away
walking by themselves
I cannot see them now

with the closing of the walkway
to the beach before nightfall
what still brings me back

on the darkened sands far
from the lights of town
is being alone there

stripped of my shorts,
shirt, and skivvies
I wade into the dark surge

wanting the waves to drench me
in their fierce caresses
to lift me

nearly take me
away from the town's lights
pull me out

like forgetfulness can
alone except for the man I passed on the walkway,
the man who eyed me (as I him)

and, unbeknownst to me,
followed me,
shed his clothes

and came naked into the whorl after me
as if he, too, wanted to wait
for the unhurried sea

to slash our thighs,
to lick us clean to the bone
as he held my hand

as the waves kept coming on,
enveloping us with the urges
of the inescapable sea.

Years After My Brother's Death

I decide to talk with him, pick
up the phone and let words
come out of me, words
locked in memory's closet, words

I spoke to him because we were born
in the same month, a year apart,
conceived when our father, an
accountant, returned for holidays–

that was during the war–from Huntsville,
San Franscisco, Chicago; put Frank Sinatra
on the phonograph; made love, and counted
January to September, one boy, two boys,

naked in the crib on the front lawn,
diapers tossed off. "Cute," neighbors
remark. One boy, two boys, learning
to write little "a" and big letter "B",

reading "*See Dick Run*," one boy,
two boys, adolescent, two watching
the *Late Show*, Frankenstein's monster
trapped, toasted in the blazing tower,

one boy, two, drunk on dates,
never home on time, with a vocabulary
of one, speaking the same words
of love frittering away with ambition.

Here I am speaking to you, my other.
You tell me death is fine, still tasting
the salt on your tongue from the Atlantic
where your son tossed your ashes.

You attest the afterlife is inexpensive,
clothing optional, no need for toilets
with the body a memory. You don't need
to make a living since you're not living,

the pace leisurely, success/failure
of equal measure. *And how am I?*
you ask. Retired from the 7 to 5,
the day what I make of it, or it of me.

The sun hikes up the slopes after me.
The day belongs to bees. Silence rides
on wings of butterflies. Your voice, what
ever I remember of it, resides between

the winter limbs and the spring wren.
One boy, two. No longer. There's
a hole in the heart where I cannot go.
Brother, speak to me again. For years

our beds nested on either side
of a nightstand and sleep,
if it took me, it took you too.
We could talk through the night,

our tales of fleeing from the police,
of fierce poker games, stalled cars,
romance gone bad. I want to say,
if you're there, *Do you remember?*

But that's not for you to do anymore.
It's for me, the one left to find words,
lift them from the time's coffin,
let them, if I listen carefully, speak.

Almost Making Love

It's morning, 10 a.m. I'm awake.
My husband offers me a tangelo.
He's snipped its skin, stripped it,
peeled it until–the firm, juicy flesh,
its thin white veins bare–piece by
piece, he slips it in my mouth,
ripe on my tongue, the tart sweet
taste of it like the sweat of his neck:
its tiny beads blossom in my throat.

Behind the Mask

It's a simple act of faith, making stuff
come alive–I slice the pumpkin's head

open, lift off the top with a brain
surgeon's deftness; the seeds, caught

in their dendrite-like strands, I scoop
out with my spoon; I carve the brainless

face into a tooth-full grin.
Then, inside I set a candle glowing

with an intelligence that surprises
me. I do all this for my three-year-old

daughter, dressed as an angel with lace
wings. I let Mr. Pumpkin perch on the doorstep

to invite in more angels. When the doorbell
rings, my daughter scoots to the front door.

It swings open to greet Dracula with blood
oozing from his lips. My daughter screams,

retreats into me. "Don't worry. It's a mask," I say.
"It's not real. See?" The older boy lifts his mask.

His white face. His gentle smile. "It's me, Matt."
Scrunched under my arm, she peeks at him,

then, at Red Riding Hood, a hobo, pirate,
Snow White, the Wicked Witch,

and Frankenstein's Monster, and offers each
a treat for their bags. That night after

the last steps clomp up to the door,
after the candle has flickered, the porch light off,

she slips into bed, but she keeps her bedroom
light on just in case more Draculas knock.

The next morning, after breakfast, she pries
open the front door. Mr. Pumpkin, gone.

To the left and right no sight of him.
Where has he gone? We find his skull

and toothless smile smashed on
Route 1. "But why, Daddy?"

I pick up one of his eyes, a perfect
triangle, hold it up as if, by gazing through

it, I could see the teens lifting him
overhead and tossing his grinning face

into oblivion. *Why?* I ask myself.
These boys weren't rising in rage against

any real threat from authority. They
weren't defying the draft, nor marching

in a holy defiance of a heathen holiday.
They are merely boys consumed with

the dumb glory of destruction. With
the carcass at my feet, my daughter,

weeping in my arms, all I can think
to do is to give Mr. Pumpkin's eye

to her, a memory of a covenant
broken now. Her face next to mine,

her tears staining my cheek, with my
promise not to worry, I say, "Honey, I don't

know. Don't know," but I do know:
the monster, unmasked, has come to life,

as real as the splattered flesh
and candle crushed beneath our feet.

False Teeth

in the glass half-filled with water,
by day a glass of water, by night what might
have preserved the brain of Einstein or the legendary
Dillinger's penis, but did hold my father's
teeth, submerged, with no tongue, no eyes,
nothing to distinguish them from thousands
of other teeth.

I picked up the glass on the sink and swished his teeth
around–I could almost hear them entice
the secretary at his office, the waitress
at the country club, or wife of his closest
friend to slip into a side room
for a quickie–could almost see his toothy smile
to win her comply. The tongue, later,
told mother nothing happened, only
a dalliance, as he poured whiskey sours,
toasted the good life, the good wife,
the good son, and the rib-eye steak
he'd sink his teeth into.

I gripped them in my hand,
almost dangling them
over a trash can, almost threatening
to never let them back in his mouth,
leaving him with a helpless gape
as if I could convince them to confess
those faithless conquests of a man
on the make. But it was too late.
They couldn't care less. He was dead.

For the Love of It

"To understand anything, you have to love it."
–Meister Eckhart

Daybreak, the sun just a sliver
as rain thuds on the porch roof,
an early June rain steadily beating
like the stomp of some ancient drum.

My daughter, still a preteen, has
her rock station beat its solid pulse
in her room, twang of guitar, strum,
thwack of a tune blending with rain.

I hear the flood slide off the roof,
engorged slippage splattering over
the deck, gouging out the gutters of debris
then charging down the hillside

by the hemlock stand at Torsy Pond,
past a cistern by a dam that contains,
in the shade, cool, clear water with
a dark skin. If you put your lips

to where the light never touches,
immutable, mysterious, it's like
kneeling before the altar of a god
long forgotten, quiet yet breathing,

as my child in her room where
the pat-a-tat of rain surely soothes her,
lets her linger in her bed as if
she dreamed us into Eden again.

The Night Skater

On Lake Ellyn, floodlights drenched the ice
with enough luminosity to lure
my mother to leave our dishes in the sink,
lace up her figure skates, and strike out
past us long-bladed boys, past couples
holding hands and skating leisurely along
to the crooning of Bing Crosby, past us all
to the center of the lake,
reserved for her alone.

In her pink skirt and skintight white
blouse, she carved a figure eight,
forward, then backward,
careful, exact, extending her arms,
she cut the eight like an incision over
and over, burrowing into the core of the lake
her mark–she was there.

Once her eight was indelible, she swung outward,
her skate's edges pressing inward,
as she easily sped past us again.
She widened her circle, once, twice,
building up speed until she leapt–suspended
in the night–turned twice and landed,
whipping around in a spin,
her arms folded across her chest,
whirling, her body a blur, round

and round and round. She
accelerated, as if no one
could stop her, as if a turbine
propelled her on.

If she had extended her arms,
she would have flown off the lake,
she would have affixed herself to the sky.

Then, with one arm out, then another,
with one skate lifted, aimed down,
she stuck the tip in the ice and stopped.

Her arms raised, she stood, her head back.
Everyone else, all us having stopped circling,
gawked in the floodlight drawn to her alone.
She had mastered this moment.

Three

EVEN OUR SHADOWS, THEIR SHADOWS, NO LONGER REMAIN.

Elegy for Time

"You can walk away
from a place but not its time."
–Richard Jackson

How many disguises have you worn?
How often have you shape-shifted
like a rabbit taken wing when
snatched from a hat? How easily
you sneak by the office of the past
and forge what has been into
the present or future tenses?

You go by many aliases: can become
at once present like a smile
appearing on an infant's face,
or past like a visionary who's
seen the candle's wax spent,
or future like the girl at the bridge
over a swollen river that keeps
enchanting her with the yet-to-be.

Is there any way for you to be
still, to let go of all your tenses,
to stem your incessant cravings to be
ambitions for your next appointed
hour, your endless have-to-dos?

I've been told there's a language
where only the now, the isness
of is, is spoken, when what has been
and what will be, all of your masks
of time, cease to matter. All
there is, all that can be, is
the rising wind in the autumn
leaves, the caress of our hand
on a lover's cheek, and the moon
like a tongue, licking our night sky.

Who we were yesterday, who
we loved last year, and where
we hanker to live next fall, have
to wait, have no place in memory's
corridors. Here I never let you shove
regret in our face, never let you
drag guilt forward to smear
the yet-to-be, never let you
lure dread into the shallow
stream of now, never let you
gag hope with a noose
of not-sures, no, never let

the aliases of the clock, those
stiff hands claw, inch by inch,
minute by minute, up the face
of hours, steal away a moment

when we could find ourselves outside
in the elements larger than we are,
in a fluid space where we could do
no harm because in futility

it stands still, hesitates,
lets ourselves be like the tide
coming up the sand, roiling
over rocks, surging, then falling
back in a whisper, lets

movement be in our stillness
of space between here and here,
and here, in the quiet of being
absolutely present like our heart
between its beats, like our day
as it turns to night, like any dream
when it wakes up to the rising wind
and the falling rain—not goodbye,
never that, but a final hello to being
here, breathing, taking us all in.

At a Drive-in Movie, 1962

Loose-lipped, maudlin, Jack Lemmon looms
on the screen. He's as drunk as I am. He's with a blonde
who's as drunk as Judy who's my date who spends
much of the movie hopping into cars with men
she doesn't know but who know more than I do.

       But that's not what I remember.

There's the refreshment stand—
a cement block building in the back
with painfully bright light and the men's room
with a long white metal trough that takes
up the whole wall for men,
               ten to twenty of us, legs
spread, hip to hip, to unzip, to tug out our cocks,
and drench the trough with torrents of urine
that disgorges down a drain at the end.

       But that's not exactly what I remember.

There is a boy, not yet five, clad in a red-booted Superman
Sleeper who stands by himself at the end of the urinal
and looks down the line of men—
some shake off their penises,
some pry them out of their underwear,
some hold them, position them,
stare at them as if they weren't their own,
while the boy looks on. On that one night,
he contemplates more of them than he's seen his whole life.

His eyes fill with delight, his mouth, a slight grin.

We look at him looking at us, and we never say a word.
                    Perhaps, he is letting us know however much
we may be ashamed of our size, afraid of our sex–
this baffling anatomy of manhood–
that in this one moment, it is alright to do what some of us
want to do: just take in the glory–shall I say it?–
the simple beauty of men's cocks–the shape, the size,
the power of our mutual urination.

Most of us keep our eyes on our own tender parts
or quickly glance to the side, counting the inches.
                But the boy just stands there, his hands at his side,
his gaze unyielding, pleased.
                            In his blue-and-red sleeper
with SUPERMAN emblazoned on his chest, he admires us,
giving us permission to witness, simply witness each other,

until his father, having finished, sees him, gently takes
his hand in his, and escorts him out into the warm night air.

August, 1956

Ginsberg types, *I saw the best minds
of my generation*. He isn't at Hastings
YMCA camp. He's in a flat across
from the Drake Hotel, zonked on peyote.
Moloch stalks the streets and swallows
children like me whole. I'm hiding
under a sheet at camp in my bunkbed.
The old weary moon haunts the sky
and casts a fist of light on me.

My first week at camp, with no TV,
I miss Ricky Nelson
with his heavy-lidded, bedroom eyes
and pouty lower lip. How he tilts his head
to tease the screeching girls.
*I'm walkin', yes, indeed
And I'm talkin',*

the song he sings I sang in my head
to bring him back to me. The moonlight
creeps up my sheets. I can hear Ricky

just as I can still hear Miss Hart drilling us
in fifth grade how to diagram a sentence,
how to fence the noun from the verb
with a vertical line and below
them a diagonal line like a slide
to hurtle *madness, starving, hysterical naked–*

words that make no sense to me as a boy
who posts postcards to Mom and Dad
I am having a good time. I swim
everyday. I can ride a horse.
Moloch howls in the hills and hankers
for us, angelic in our BVDs before bedtime
as we wag our weenies goodnight in the nippy
night air and slip under our sheets.

Ginsberg, thirty by then, crazed and visionary,
released from an insane asylum, clear across
the continent from Lake Villa, Illinois, is bedeviled
by his own nightmares and how the *incarnate gaps*
in Time & Space are dashed out of his consciousness
as if he too is frightened of what
Moloch might do to him
as well as to us. "August, 1956"

isn't just the title to this poem.
It's when I want Ricky
right by my side, whispering,
"Pretty baby, I'm waitin'."

The moon nibbles on my cheek.
Barely heard, Ginsberg is bent
over me, his large glasses perched
low on his nose. He lets me know
he is writing about a life
I have yet to live, laying out
each sentence in his journal as I would
later in mine, illuminating *men who howled*

on their knees in the subway and were
dragged off the roof waving genitals and manuscripts.

Do his lines still confound me? His howl
is like a mosquito at the screen, inches
away that will take decades
to reach me because

all I dream of is Ozzie and
Harriet who have picked Ricky
and me up in their powder-blue
Packard and drive us past the *saintly*
motorcyclist and *public parks*
far from the *negro streets* to our safe
suburban home where, cross-legged,
transfixed before the TV, we watch ads
for Moloch's latest Hotpoint refrigerator.

Ricky looks right at me as if he
has heard Ginsberg whisper
and better understands
we must wake from
this merciless dream
of this life that never belonged to us
as if he understands, too late,
how our lives could end
like Ricky's did, consumed
in flames, as if he lit
an angry fix.

– Italicized text from "Howl" by Allen Ginsberg
and "I'm Walkin'" by Fats Domino, (as performed by Ricky Nelson)

Tell the World

When I spin
the stack of 45s back to 1958
in seventh grade at the heart hop,
Nancy Short, the redhead hankering
for a boy with the right moves, asks me
to dance to Elvis's "Wear My Ring
Around Your Neck." My saddle shoes
aren't like Elvis's blue suede shoes,
my white dress shirt can't compete
with his slick gold Lamé suit,
but she offers her hand to me
and I take it.
                Her arms reach
around my waist, her breast
presses to my chest. She clutches
me as if she's staked claim
on a man who can dance
her to the moon.
                Elvis's voice,
deep and sexy, tells me *she's*
mine as we shuffle back and
forth, hip to hip, the friction
enough to light the gym.
                When the stylus
slips, clinks, and lifts, she brushes
her lips soft and tender on my cheek

                  that right then,
as if by the magic of his baritone,
ceases to be my cheek but morphs
into Elvis's cheek, as are my hips,
his hips, my shirt, his hot pink shirt,
my hair, his combed back pompadour,
                  but the microphone,
grasped in my hand, is mine as I bow
to the left where lonely boys glower
in disbelief, to the front where my teacher
applauds, and to the right where the girls'
screams rip across the gym floor.
                  I jog down the exit ramp
to my pink Cadillac limousine that will drive
me far away from the women who want me
more than I will ever want them. Here alone
in the quiet backseat I contrive
new lyrics, and breathless,
croon this top-ten hit.

Pat Boone, the Naked Lady, and Me

Why do I keep coming back to the basement?
My parents gone to another cocktail party,
I put on the 45s of Pat Boone, his latest hits,
until his voice fills the wood-paneled room.

Word by word, I sing each phrase with him,
a duet, two clean-cut guys, bemoaning how
every star's a wishing star that shines
for you. I have no idea who you are. Or if
there will ever be a you. I think of Michael,
his cheek so close to mine, the way he slipped
right through my fingers. I flip the records.
Ain't that a shame. I had *done [him] wrong.*

Beneath two squinty windows, Pat and I
commiserate by ourselves in a room
with a bar with fifths of Gordon's Gin,
vermouth, a cutting board for limes,
and rows of Scotch, bourbon, vodka.

Above them hangs a naked lady in a bathtub,
her toe in the spigot, water spraying
over her belly and breasts as if, with enough
martinis and Old Fashioneds, she might cease
to be a painting and alight on the barstool
right next to me. As each 45 plays,
I memorize the lines like I'm Pat.

He doesn't care that he has to sing these songs
over and over, because in his pure baritone,
he knows it is just the two of us, there
on the *Moody River*. He knows we are
more deadly than the vainest knife. He knows
no one can live with a severed heart.

And as we keep on singing about our
being the one to blame, about our *broken
hearts*, the naked lady leans over the bar,
pats my hand, sings a few bars with us,
then says, "Nice voice, kid. Here's to you,"
and pours me a tall, iced glass of sadness.

–Italicized text in from "Every Star Is a Wishing Star,"
"Ain't That a Shame," and "Moody River" by Pat Boone

Photo of My Father as a Boy

The photo is formal. Posed. Sepia, 1925.
He's impeccably dressed as he always was,
sitting on a window seat in a jacket, white shirt,
tie, and long trousers like the corporate executive
he would become, his hair trimmed above his ears,
and long on the top, combed straight back
as it would be his whole life.

He's young, maybe ten, he must know he's special
enough to have the Rose Studio in Champaign, Illinois,
photograph him, the boy seen in town as Howard's,
the boy who clears tables, fills water glasses at one
of his dad's restaurants, where ladies remark,
"What a handsome boy, so grown-up."

He doesn't realize that in ten years, his father will be
bankrupt (the Depression)—and working as a welfare
agent in Ohio. He doesn't know that as a freshman
at Ohio State, he'll come home one afternoon to find
his mother, Lulu, splayed on the oven door, gas still on.

But he'll remember this jacket with a flap and button
on the chest pocket. He'll remember what it means
to look right—"Such a stylish dresser. What good taste"—
say the ladies to this suit jacket that carries the boy
into the man, the man into success; to this jacket
that commutes to work each morning, exits at corporate
headquarters, and comes back to his wife at night.

When I was five, he took me to Marshall Fields,
to be measured and pinned—sleeves at the wrists,
cuffs at shoe top, shoulders drawn up and in—I was
his boy looking right, photographed each holiday,
as he used to say, "dressed to kill" as if appearances
could untether the man from the corpse.

Better dressed, better looking than any
other kids at the club, I learned his lesson well.
Yes. I tried to look right—to marry, have kids,
get jobs bigger than I was—to pull the knot
of the tie, hold the thin end, and weave the wide
end over, back, up, and down, tugging so tight
against my throat, I almost gagged.

For thirty years, I kept wearing the tie,
the shirt, the slacks, and the jacket, a closet
full of them—the tweed, the blazer, the blue
pin-striped suits—thinking that all together,
they'd make me the man I was supposed to be:

the straight man, not the man who loved feeling
the salesmen's expert hands pulling the tape
from my shoulders to my wrist, from my ankles
to my crotch, as they measured my body to fit me
into the right identity, the one their tender hands
could so easily undo.

It has taken me twenty years to ...
I was going to say "defy" or even "shirk,"
but since I'm divorced, and remarried, this time to
a man, if I said those words, I would be lying.

It's time to admit that in my closet,
on two rods, hang fourteen jackets all with
matching slacks, shirt, and, yes, ties.
I keep them hostage even as, month by month,
in my T-shirt and jeans, I'm no longer the man
I was. I no longer need to look right ...

yet the jackets remain, rarely coming out.
Their silence reminds me, no matter
how far I push away your image
of me, Dad, I'm still your son.

Back to 6 Saint Charles Street

What was I looking for?
Some frayed cloth of childhood?
My coming down two flights of stairs
to the Christmas tree by that window?
The latticed window in the attic
where I spied on Mrs. Wolfe, the witch
who lopped off the heads of peonies?
Those steps from the back door
into the kitchen where mother
baked cinnamon buns and brewed
a pot of coffee?

       Lost in my memory,
I never saw the owner, hands on hips,
staring at me. "Is there a problem?" he asked.
I told him I once lived there.
"When was that?" He studied me.
"Oh, twenty. No, not that. Good God!
Nearly forty years ago."
He asked, "Forty?"
Could I have been away that long?

I didn't want to bother him,
but he insisted, took me in the side door
to more rooms and more wallpaper and more stairs,
first one flight, then another, deep
into the vault of yesterday. He kept asking,
"Is this familiar?" as I touched the banister,
looked in a room where a TV now rested
where my brother and I had once slept.

With this stranger guiding me, I became
a somnambulist undreaming my childhood
that, even as I tried, didn't come back
any closer to me, but seemed like a ship
unmoored from a pier, and drifting far
from shore, how it kept drifting farther
from me as I tried to yank it back.

We sat at the kitchen table and drank coffee.
His wife had gone shopping with their two kids,
both boys, four and five,
who were, as did my brother and I,
living in my house of memory
where we had slid down the banister
and flopped headlong on the carpet.

But it was their home now,
where rooms would shelter them
within their walls for a time,
whatever time they had,
and then would let them go to take
that home with them into memory's dominion.

I don't remember what the owner and I said,
his being a young father, my being an elder.
But, as I stood by the doorway,
he opened his arms to give me a hug
as my mother would have done
before telling me, dressed as I was
in my David Crockett coonskin cap,
"Go on now. Go out and play."

A Duet: Morning Song

In the morning when the doves coo
back and forth from cage to cage,
the light nestles against the wainscotting.
Light seems to be dozing, at ease, quiet
as if it could stay there for a lifetime, its
bright splotches fragmented through
the window grilles, boxed, squared,
evenly framed up the wall and half
way along the floor. Light presses down,
casting warmth over Pepper,
our rat terrier, his belly exposed,
his head lolled back, content on this
March day when even the caged birds
sing, when history quiets, when those
at war might put down their arms and lift
their faces to the light that extends
itself like a long arm and says, "Now,
now," as if to comfort us, to let us know
today is enough. Even now, love,
ever elusive, ever in search of its
home, is reaching though the window
like the light, extending itself to us.

Evening Song

In the evening the light from the lamp
leans across my shoulder and down
the hallway. The dark dulls the paintings.
In the doorway, blackness. Here is the quiet
susurration of a decade-old lab.
Otherwise, a silence–no birds
singing, only the faint sound of a distant
car. Now the deeper enveloping dark is
drawn to the couch, to the end table with
a half-empty cup of coffee, stacks
of *New Yorker* magazines, and the last
plants I keep by the window for winter
as if this one plain lamp light were enough,
were all that prevents oblivion, that slow,
incessant rupture with reality. The long
shadow under my hand lifts, descends,
and follows each word I write as if
vigilant, watchful, making sure each
word carries the weight of its own
darkness. How each of us casts our
own shadow, some elemental visceral
essence that lets us hold as long as we
can this living, this late lingering light.

3 a.m.

I wake to the silence of the hour. I'm no age.
The room's ink black, undreamed.

In these hours, on the edge of my bed,
I might be 15. My parents' breath across the hall:
my father's stentorian, nasal gasp,
my mother's quiet, beelike hum.

I have homework. A chemistry book, opened to an unread
page. I'll read it in the morning. My brother, in bed across
from me, dreams a dream that swallows him
inside the dark as if time, hungry, had devoured

fifty years. I can no longer find him,
nor my father who collapsed on a floor
decades ago–a fighter with nothing left.
Mother's no longer in any room.
My children have moved far from home.

Must I wake to this life that has been?

Water creeps up the beach and laps at the foundations.
The black lab nestles next to me, deep in her own dream.
She yelps, chases a long-eared rabbit into a thicket.

My lover moans on the other side of the bed.
Tomorrow will soon tap on our window.
It won't ask what happened to me.

For now, I know what I never know
in daylight, when the asters bloom
after the hard frost and the bees
rummage in petals for nectar:
what matters are those breathing
here beside me, this world
I never want to leave.

It Goes Like This

We were drunk, standing outside the White Castle,
holding the smallest, most tasteless burger on Earth.
My best friend asked if I ever wondered
about the stars and what was beyond them—
if there was an end to it all?

I gulped down my burger, soggy with onions, in one bite.

Neon lights washed across my friend's face,
swaying as he was, back and forth, staring
and pointing at the immensity above us.
"Think of it." he said, "What we're seeing
can't be half of it. And if that's so,
how far does it go before it ends?"

I took a bite of my second burger. It was already gone,
not the universe—the vast *out there*—that kept
expanding and reaching, getting bigger
and bigger despite my offering my friend
a tiniest cardboard cup of French fries.

He ate one and shook his head as though,
if he shook it right, if he could rearrange
the clutter of his brain to explain, he could
reconfigure a world that spun around the sun,
that spun within a galaxy that revolved in a
universe swirling inside his sixteen-year-old brain.

I sucked the last onions from my last burger.
We sauntered across the street, my friend
still gazing at the sky, that, for all I knew,
was looking back at us, waiting for our answer.

We went to the dance at Dayne Street school
where 45s, one after another, spun on the record player.
We danced "The Twist." We spun up and down,
around the room, to Chubby Checker wailing,
Yeaah! Twist again like we did last summer,
come on let's twist again like we did last year,
as if the needle, caught in its groove, caused us,
and everyone around us, to circle the floor.

Some couples seemed to be grooving, really hummin'
in their own galaxy, while others like my friend
and me circulated like planets through the dark
immensity of the gym. We drifted in and out
of the dance, waiting for the Beatles to sing,
You know, you twist so fine . . . come on
and twist a little closer now. Then we danced
again as if the universe had suddenly changed
its mind, reversed itself—*let me know that*
you're mine—and contracted into us. Just us.

–Italicized text from "The Twist" by Chubby Checker
and "Twist and Shout" by the Beatles

All for the Taking

When I was old enough to understand
I was different but not old enough to know why,
an older neighbor, Mr. Robinson, took a fancy
to my solitary nature and invited me to help him
with his garden, set, as it was, on a hillside.
There I saw row after row of grapevines,
trellised, tall; raspberries lodged between
railroad ties; corn with squash twined around
its stalks; and rows of beans, carrots, beets, onions,
lettuce–all for the taking–and out back,
three plum trees with smooth gray trunks.

When the plum's white buds blossomed in April,
we inspected them, saw the first green nubs, and–

I know what you're thinking, this man,
this young boy, but that's not this story, not at all–

that summer, after we had weeded each row;
after we had picked fistfuls of carrots;
after we had entered his basement, steered
his Lionel trains–*hoot-hoot*–
through little towns telescoping
into tunnels; after I had slipped into
his darkroom as he rinsed the wet paper,
dipping it in one bath, then another,
the red light barely enough for me
to discern the image of rosebuds, corn husks,
plum buds blooming on the page–
after that, we walked out to the trees.

He lifted me up to pluck a purple plum,
and let me down to take the first bite,
juice on my chin. He took the next
bite until there was just the pit left.

The next blank paper in the bath would be
the image of me holding that plum.
But it was not only an image,
it was really the sweet flesh
of the plum, of a tree filled with them,
and the taste of the jam his wife
made from them, and the memory
of that taste on toast in the morning
that I held onto for years.
On that day, her jam tasted just
as fresh as that plum once had been.

Always, I remember how he held the plum
out to me, and how, when I bit into it
and savored its flesh, he smiled,
as, I have come to see, God did
on the third day at all the plants
that bore fruit and seeds—his own creations—
when he said, knowing as all good gardeners
like Mr. Robinson knew, that *this was good*.

Sunday Morning, Late September

The peach stewed in oatmeal—
golden flesh in a blue bowl.

It's a bright, clear day—
Mount Pisgah, a far-off blue-gray

in the early morning light.
No one's left for church.

The road's a hushed black.
The dogs lie on the cool grass.

I sit in my T-shirt and night shorts,
barefoot. This day seventy-one

years ago, at 6 a.m., I claimed the air.
Now, off in the distance, hovering,

lifted on updrafts, four hot air
balloons, brightly colored

reds and blues, drift across
the heedless sky, peaceful as I.

Twelve pounds of terrier pup
nestles against my leg. I skritch his neck.

He dashes off, prancing with a stick
like a scepter. He's King of the World.

The balloons are still close enough
for me to hear the blasts of their burners

and see each one lift gently
like a wish. I listen to the cardinals

at the feeder I just filled, gleeful,
sunflower seeds in their beaks. They leave

a red-tinged feather an inch long
on my lap. If there's something

like prayer in this waiting
for nothing in particular, this

being given over to caws of crows
in a distant tree or the balloons

receding to mere dots like punctuation
marks on the horizon,

if there's God in any of this, some luminous
being who's waiting for a hush

in the din of bombastic politicians
declaiming their significance

to the air, then perhaps the two
of us are waiting here, older

by years we need not measure,
but present to what's quiet

in the slow accretion of light
that has almost reached us here.

Four

IT IS AN ILLUSION THAT WE
WERE EVER ALIVE,

LIVED IN THE HOUSE OF
MOTHERS, ARRANGED
OURSELVES

BY OUR OWN MOTIONS
IN THE FREEDOM OF AIR.

Little Voice on a Suicide Help Line

like a pup behind a shut door,
a whimper so small
it barely quivers
in the phone's speaker.

Ear pressed to the receiver,
I listen hard.

Me: *Is there something
you want?*
You: Not a word.
Me: *You want to die?*
You: A thin yes. A pause.
Me: *That way? Now?*
You: Yes. Tiny like a mustard seed.
Me: *You are all right. We all have
such feelings. Do you know that?*
You: No, a single word again.

For an hour—No. Yes. No.—
I feel like you're under glass,
sinking deeper into
a coffin of silence

and I reach out with my words,
words, words as if one
could shatter the spell,
set you free.

Are you listening?
I'm still trying to reach you.

Keep Running

Deep into the night, I ran.
I had no idea how far
nor how long
but I ran into the teeth
of a winter wind,
my breath clouded
before me.
My running shoes stung
on the icy pavement.
The headlights stabbed the air.
For hours my body plodded
the miles from my home,
miles from a wife
at a door who had asked,
"Where are you going?"
I had no idea where I was
going. All I wanted was out,
pushing myself to stride faster
down a trail by the woods
into the past
where I was no one,
just a sophomore alone,
with a chemistry book
with elements arranged
in order, in rows,
just a breath in a room
in the dark, the stillness
absolute, not seeking
anyone, sitting at a desk

with a pen and the blank
page of a journal that led
back into a question I could
not outrace no matter how far
I ran from myself into a life
I should have lived
miles and miles away.

The Ghost of Frank O'Hara

"… the waves have kept me from reaching you."
– From "To the Harbormaster" by Frank O'Hara

I'd walked that Fire Island beach
halfway to Cherry Grove before
the ocean disrobed beside me,
sand the color of mahogany.
O'Hara had stood where I was,

where, as the driver of the jeep said,
"He was walking towards me ….
He didn't even try to move, he just
kept on walking." The jeep struck him
with such force he left a dent.

O'Hara had lain right here, a few steps
from me, liver ruptured,
leg shattered, 40 hours to live.

His friends wondered why he kept
walking toward the jeep. Maybe
it was because he was drunk–
it was 2:30 a.m.–or because
he saw a welcoming, a way out
of non-writing, his being fed up
with being too well-known.
Why not walk into a gift
even if it's coming
at twenty-five miles per hour?

Why not walk toward the lights?

I had just been to a tea dance,
to chance I might strike someone's
fancy, someone who'd dance
a dance with me.

Alone, the summer newly upon me,
I passed through O'Hara's ghost
and felt him latch onto my arm, ask,
"What are you doing here?"
He spoke about how gay men get by,
for he loved language and I liked
listening as he went on and on,
never stopped, his sinewy, birdlike
body loping down the beach.

He had an advantage over me
since he had never aged, never
collapsed in a stupor in his fifties
with lung cancer or cirrhosis.
He looked much younger than me,
striding faster than I was toward a light,
except this time the light was
my weekend rental with a balcony
and a view he and I would soon share
while white waves advanced quickly,
these massive overtures rising up,
and crashing down as his voice—
for I was still listening—
became the voice of the sea.

Sandsprit Park

Maybe it was the wood stork with its toothpick legs,
or the brown pelican with its schoolmaster's gaze,
or the funereal cormorant with its wings extended.
Certainly not the black vulture draping the sky,
nor the sludge brown tidal waters suffocating
the bluenose dolphins and spotted sea trout.
Still whatever it was drew my Mother to Sandsprit Park
where the St. Lucie River, Indian River Lagoon,
and Atlantic Ocean inlet coalesced into swirling,
ever-shifting currents, tugging one another
in, then out again.

Week after week, year after year at sundown,
she and her friend Jean would take their martinis
and sit under the palms by the pier
to watch the boats, rigged for deep-sea fishing,
gunning out of the inlet and, hours later,
idling in with their catch. Just two elderly ladies,
fixtures by then, waving at the fishermen
who waved back as pelicans, avid for bait,
hovered over the incoming boats, and gulls
cried out hungrily, swooped to snatch
the cast off entrails in the white wakes.

Sometimes, a heron high-stepped in the shallows
by the shore. Some nights the massive backs
of manatees rose up and passed by the dock,
their mammoth mouths scrounging seagrass,
hugging the shore lined by the mangroves.

Jean informed mom about Mr. Shaw who was,
once again, having an affair with a club's waitress.
Mother said, "Poor girl. She has no taste."
They laughed and sipped and took it all in—
the sun stretched across the palms,
the wild parrots gossiping in the wind.
For years, they gathered there before Jean
entered elder care and left mom alone.

Yet even after my mother had fallen, even when
I had to care for her, help her with her walker,
she came back with me, our iced teas in hand
to Sandsprit Park where the sun napped in the inlet
and the boat's wake lapped against a piling
where a lone pelican perched and gazed,
like Mother, at the blue-green infinity.

Then, eyes down, wary of fissures in the wood,
Mother said, "Time to go," and moved the walker
forward as I watched the water behind her
flow out to the ocean. In an hour or two, both
of us knew the tide would turn and come
back again, and the pelican would lift off
the piling, swoop down on his extended wings,
and skim over the waves effortlessly, his long
bill packed like a suitcase before him.

Memorial

In the lapse of evening light, snow falls on the shoulders
of a statue. It's a man ready with a rifle, his finger
on the trigger, and in his other hand, the forestock
covered inch-high with a rim of snow. He's in a park
with two benches blanketed in snow, a memory
of war on a pedestal. Of the Civil War?
Or WWI? The plaque's indecipherable.
His helmet seems like a far-off planet with its ring of white.
He's wintered here for eight decades, or more.

Lights from two stores leak onto the street.
Nothing moves. Fall has surrendered to winter.
In windows, a blue flicker of TVs illuminates yards.

The nose of the soldier looks as if he's
plastered it with zinc oxide. The carcass
of a Christmas tree, laced with strings
of popcorn, leans against a picket fence.
A house sparrow nips at the popcorn.

I stand in the middle of the street.
Too late for traffic. Quiet has settled
here, no marks of tires, the street,
unpeopled, rivered in white. Only me
and the soldier, the lights, and the bird.

A car honks–the driver
shoots out, "Watch it" and plows by.

I slip yet step out of the way
onto the sidewalk, right under the soldier
who is gazing a long way off as if
he's seen the enemy coming
or, perhaps, comrades waiting by a fire,
their faces aglow, their hands pressed
to the flames, beckoning him home.

Useless

In the bottom drawer of memory,
my first lover presses his cheek
near mine, utters breathlessly,
"I'll love you forever." Decades

later, his words are useless
like boxes of photos whose faces
no longer register, or tires
without treads, or branches

without leaves. Seems there's
nothing worth holding onto.
Yet there's still the scent of his
cologne, his lips on mine,

his hand in my once-long hair
clinging like that one leaf,
after the cold, grips a limb
as if assured, deep within,

a sweetness will rise, infuse
the green anatomy with not
as much memory of the past,
but an incarnation of being

alive, the feel of him on me,
the usefulness of skin to us.

In a Wicker Couch on the Back Porch

with our daughter and son asleep upstairs,
my wife wanted us to talk in private.

A comforter, folded, covered her knees.
She said, "This may hurt."

No dagger in her hand, only words about
a woman, a lawyer at her office,

about love unexpected, how she had fallen
for her. She asked if I was cold and snugged

the comforter onto my knees. A few leaves
hung from an oak, the unwilling, trenchant.

She said she was "sorry" so many times
the word echoed inside itself like a drum.

"How much time do you need?" she asked.
I said, "How about a year?"

That was when she cried and wiped
her face with her sleeve.

I asked if she loved her, and she nodded.
"We need to tell the children," I said.

"In time," she said. "All in due time."
In due time, I thought, as if we owed

time something, as if the emptiness
pressing in on me was its price.

We hugged and she left me there thinking.
I wandered to the deck, down the hillside,

beyond the hemlocks and the white birch
to a shallow stream that marked the property's edge.

There, nothing stirred. I couldn't hear her footfalls
upstairs in our bedroom. I couldn't hear our children

rustle in their beds, nor the dog on the slate
floor. In due time—I couldn't figure what else

to do—I returned to those sounds,
climbed each stair, counting them

like the steps to a guillotine,
the blade already tracing my neck.

I stripped, slipped on my pajamas,
lifted the covers, and slid back in

as I had done for twenty-five years,
there beside her. Familiar fingers

fretted my back. "Are you …
are you all right?"

Our First Orbit

We could see the carnival lights
collapsing in the falling waves
as we rose from the platform–
my seven-year-old daughter and me
in a mini airplane. Her body squinched against mine,
my arms folded over hers as the machine,
grinding its engine into gear, began to
spin. Tethered to only a cable, we picked up
speed, whirling outward, dipping down, then flung
up, pilotless as the red and yellow lights splattered
on the darkening beach below. When my daughter said,
"I'm going to be sick," I told her to breathe because,
nearly sick myself, I needed to maintain
control. I told her to focus on something,
anything unmoving, focus on the steering wheel
that, even in the grips of centrifugal force, stayed still.
Not like me, propelled so fast I felt I'd passed,
then caught up with myself and from there,
had traveled beyond my body, in a whirling
so fast, it cut time loose until my life seemed
to trail behind me. But then I felt my hand
around hers steady on the wheel, my stomach
in my throat, her head against my chest,
both of us unleashed together from gravity,
two astronauts flying into the stratosphere, out
to a galaxy, yet unnamed, where we held on
to each other, just held on as if we were already home.

First Date After Coming Out at 48

Past the age when sex should matter less,
here I was with my first boyfriend,
a man my age who cooked dinner for me–
I forget what it was–and afterward, we sat on
a couch by the fireplace with cups of custard.

Mine done, I did what I had never dared to do:
put my hand on his thigh, right there.
He gobbled the last bites of his dessert.
Then, as instantly as a crew member
on the spaceship Enterprise, I felt my body
transported to his bedroom where we did
what I had always wanted to do.
My pleasure erupted out of me like ecstasy
reclaiming its etymology.

In the end, I wanted to beam my body up,
wanted to keep feeling that sweet transport
from Earth to pleasure, but he, old hand
at piloting men back to Earth, took out
his hand towels and wiped up the evidence,
wiped us so clean we looked as if nothing
had happened when I wanted it to happen
again and again and again without anyone
stopping us–wanted love to hurtle me
at warp speed from one galaxy into another.

The Breath of a Wing

The zebra finch flutters by my face—
the air tactile, featherlike.

In the emptiness of day, I sit
in a brown leather La-Z-Boy.

A dove coos, *I'm here, I'm here.*
Who was it who said the world

was with God? Or was it the Word
is God? I'm not sure.

But Blake did say words have
their own divinity. They reach

yet fail to reach yet reach to
where I am here with my lover.

The purple lilacs leave
their scent like wings.

This day is like all the others,
as we, too, are like all others.

Our four dogs sleep on the carpet.
It's midday. Much of light

has spent its soft dominion
over the wall. The caged finches

sing one to another, *Watch me*.
They flit from perch to perch.

Dazzling, persistent in flight,
they aren't hurried, yet flick

off the lights at night, and they settle
as the pulse under the skin

Where no words exist. Indwelling
Heidegger called it, the way words

dwell in the here, the perch, the nest,
the window, the raucous sky. My lover once

touched my cheek like the breath of a wing
and whispered, "I love you," so near me

the words like a tongue
flamed in my mouth.

Barrier Islands, St. Petersburg, Florida, 1952

Dawn lipped the palms. The lightness
of waves no higher than a shoe
and quiet as a prayer lapped
against our thighs as my brother
and I waded past one sandbar after another
far out in the illimitable blue-green.
We plucked from one sandbar
anemones and conchs, still living. We saw
how the waves sucked them under,
sand sloshing over them, then pulling
back, exposing us to them again,
their shells glistening jewels.

Our plastic pails packed with these
treasures, we stomped back to The Sands,
my brother, quick of step, yards ahead
to offer Mom, "Look what I got."
She'd been waiting for us on the balcony, ever
watchful, wary, and now she picked each
from the bucket, flicked off the sand,
boiled them, scooped out their innards,
and let them dry there on the windowsill.

In those months, we plundered plenty,
not once thinking of ourselves as thieves
in a jewelry store whose owner
was pouring rings, watches, and necklaces
worth a fortune into our buckets.
We simply took as if this were our destiny.

For years, my family left every one of those keepsakes
to disintegrate on our shelves or dropped them,
mere powder, in one move or another
like my brother and mother whose ashes
we dispersed, as they wished, into the Gulf.

Yet the light that tripped over waves
and spent its first liquid warmth
on us and the breakers that chased
us to the shore before they retreated–
all these keep coming back to me
as if what we were after, two brothers
chest-high in water, crawling on our hands
and knees to grapple with the churning surf,
were not those shells but just being there
inside the gold accretion of each new day.

The Long Walk

Along the path by Bent Creek, early when the light
first leans between the firs and hickories, first shimmers
on the waters lulling by the bridge, we walk with our terriers.

They tug and stick their noses in the underbrush, lift
their legs, to let others know, "We've been here,"
and we, too, admit that need, to attest,
"We have walked here together," the miles
side by side, two men, gripping these leashes.

In time, as the light lifts higher, the mist rises,
and reveals coming at us, an elderly couple,
one with ski poles to keep his balance, his wife,
wary, close by, yet halting often, also gazing
at those eddies, hearing, as she waits,
the wish of sound the water makes.

We wave and merely say, "Good morning,"
as we pass. In a few years, with my knees
as they are and the sore hip, we may be
strolling as they are—not making time,
but walking still, finding some solace
in this quiet, these taut leashes, and this love,
yes, love we find in walking together.

Do Flowers Die No Matter What?

My mother used to cut flowers, fistfuls,
then arranged them, carefully blending
reds with muted yellows, greens to frame
her display. In a week, I'd find the blossoms
wrecked, wilted petals on our divan.
What was the use of cutting a flower?
Beauty with a gash in its stem?

Yet still undaunted, on some evenings,
after tossing out the dead, she'd pluck
fresh blooms from fields, from gardens,
from anywhere they grew, and stem by
stem, arrange them anew.

Here I am, seven decades on, picking words
from my brain, sticking them together, knowing
full well they might last no longer than flowers
in a vase. I want to stop such foolishness.
Who will ever remember what I wrote?

I'm no Whitman with his *twenty-eight young men
bathing by the shore*. No Eliot with his *unreal city*.
No Crane with his *infinite consanguinity*.

No Ginsberg with his *best minds … destroyed by madness.*
I might be more like Emily in her bog–
or like the eye atop the unfinished pyramid
on a dollar bill, little, unilluminated,
wishing I were worth more. Why do I
keep on holding up my time to the light,
fastening myself to this page, as if my own
life might be worth remembering?

Should I have remembered lives more significant–
whole species extinct, whole regions desiccated
as dust, whole cities rioting, whole people
threatened and stripped of their rights?

Yet my black lab, thirteen now, groans
and extends her paws to me. The pendulum bob
of my grandfather clock swings back and forth.
My memory, so alert to who I was, has almost
forgotten who I am. None of this may matter.

My significance may be like the drawer where
I keep the many-colored socks I have almost
stopped wearing or like hundred-dollar
Cole-Haan shoes, still polished yet dusty,
restless, useless on my shelf.

But the me who was angry at being me is
no longer me. He is long gone. I do not
resent as much as I lament losing him.
I keep on trying to write him back
to life the way mom kept on bringing
the blossoms inside as if, by gathering
them into a bouquet, and by leaving
them so near us, our bright whole
world would at last come alive.

CREDITS

I am most appreciative to the editors of these publications, where these poems, sometimes in different forms, first appeared.

"Almost Making Love," *Monterey Poetry Review*

"A Duet: Morning Song. Evening Song," *Soup Can Magazine*

"A Summer without Mosquitoes," *Beltway Poetry Quarterly*

"Barrier Islands" and "What We Remembered When Father Lay Dying," *Garfield Lake Review*

"Father, There Was a Time" and "Years After My Brother's Death" *Sand Hills Literary Magazine*

"For the Taking," *Evening Street Review*

"It Goes Like This," *Poet's Choice Anthology: Drunken Moments*

"Man on the Walkway," *Carolina Bard Anthology*

"Night Figure Skater," *Kalopsia Literary Review*

"Sunday Morning, Late September," *Without a Doubt: poems illuminating faith (New York Quarterly)*

"The Breath of a Wing," *Stoneboat Literary Journal*

"The Day Marilyn Died," *The Bangalore Review*

"The First Orbit," *Red River Review*

"The Ghost of Frank O'Hara," *Muleskinner Review*

"The Long Walk," *Isotrope Literary Journal*

"Useless," *Asheville Poetry Review*

ACKNOWLEDGMENTS

The mythic notion that a poet, alone in a garret, slaves into the night, worrying words on the page, makes for a good scene in a movie about some troubled soul. But in real life, most poets perfect their craft with the help of others, many of whom are close friends and form a community of artists. They work together to workshop their poems, doing their best to make drafts become finished poems.

What I have realized is that poetry generates images and associations and, yes, communities that reach into our hearts. The images inside us are like talismans that, if we press our fingers to them, feeling the heat of their symbolic power, will spark some memory, will, if we trust it, let it speak, will not just be a memory but an epiphany, a realization that something magical has happened. We cannot evade that realization, nor can we ignore it, since it wants to tell us something that we have not known or seen before and is something that will change our life and make us who we are. As such, poems are not so much made by us as much as we are made by poems. We come to find our true selves in poems. And I would add, we come to find ourselves in the community of poets who have come to know us.

I have been blessed to have many writers' groups over the years. These groups have read my poems and given me sage advice about how to improve what I write.

The poems in this book are better because they cared enough about them to demand I make each word, each line, each stanza live up to a standard of excellence.

When my poems are raw, first completed, I send them to my lifelong friend and wordsmith, Nancy McDaniel, who combs the text finding those inevitable knots where my dyslexia weaves its way into my writing and teases them out.

I offer, therefore, my thanks to my Maine compatriots Betsy Sholl, Marita O'Neill, Linda Aldrich, Gibson LeBlanc, and Colin Cheney for their amazing understanding of what makes a poem work.

In Asheville, North Carolina, I am indebted to Alida Woods, Janet Ford, Norma Bradly, Ruth Hoffman, Kathy Nelson, and Stephanie Biziewski for their incisive comments.

I am also grateful for three poets for reviewing my manuscript, giving me advice on what should stay, what needed revision, and what should be cut. Betsy Sholl who has a keen eye for detail gave me wonderful advice about pruning poems and eliminating the dross. Dawn Potter, who offers a workshop, "Chapbook Seminar," was instrumental in helping devise a structure for the book. Marie Harris suggested changes that shaped the manuscript.

I am also grateful for Warren Publishing for their meticulous assistance in making this book come to life. In particular, I tip my hat to Amy Klein whose meticulous editing and reshaping of the book brought it to a new level that I could never have achieved without her brilliant sense of language and structure. I also appreciate the care, sensitivity, and insight that Amy Ashby demonstrated in refining and making sure from interior to cover this book represented what it should to make it work.

I am indebted to Mindy Kuhn for her envisioning, designing, and incorporating the cover and interior artwork.

This book would not be as it is without Liz Kalloch's artwork. Her artwork makes this book achieve what true art aspires to be: beautiful. In case you want to look at more of her work, Liz Kalloch is an abstract multimedia artist who paints, writes, lives, and works in Maine. You can find more of her artwork at lizkallochfineart.com.

This book would never be what it is today without them. My deepest thanks to all of them!

www.ingramcontent.com/pod-product-compliance
Lightning Source LLC
Chambersburg PA
CBHW041719090426
42739CB00019B/3488